Hidden word sudoku

Hidden word sudoku

The last word in sudoku puzzles

Robin Wilson

Sterling Publishing Co., Inc.
New York

The right of Robin Wilson to be identified as the author of this book has been asserted in accordance with the Copyright, Designs and Patents Act 1988.

10 9 8 7 6 5 4 3 2 1

Published in 2006 by Sterling Publishing Co., Inc.
387 Park Avenue South, New York, NY 10016

First published in 2005 by The Infinite Ideas Company Limited
36 St. Giles, Oxford, England OX1 3LD
© 2005 by The Infinite Ideas Company Limited

Distributed in Canada by Sterling Publishing
C/o Canadian Manda Group, 165 Dufferin Street
Toronto, Ontario, Canada M6K 3H6

Sterling ISBN-13: 978-1-4027-3818-0
      ISBN-10: 1-4027-3818-8

For information about custom editions, special sales, premium and corporate purchases, please contact Sterling Special Sales Department at 800-805-5489 or specialsales@sterlingpub.com.

Designed and typeset by Baseline Arts Ltd, Oxford

Contents

Preface

The sudoku craze has become an epidemic. A type of puzzle that few people had heard of a year ago has become a worldwide phenomenon.

Much of the reason for sudoku's popularity stems from the fact that its basic rules are so very simple – given a 9 x 9 grid divided into nine 3 x 3 mini-grids (boxes) and with some entries already placed in it, fill in the rest of the grid in such a way that no character appears twice in the same row, column or box.

In spite of the appearance of numbers in many sudoku puzzles, no calculations are required – these are not arithmetic puzzles but logical ones, requiring only logical thinking, patience, and perseverance. To emphasize this, some puzzles feature letters or other symbols, rather than the numbers from 1 to 9 that appear in most sudoku puzzles.

Dozens of sudoku puzzle books have appeared in the past few months, devoted entirely to letter puzzles. These 'hidden word' puzzles have an extra feature – when you complete one of them, a hidden nine-letter word or phrase will appear in one of the rows, columns or boxes.

If you wish to improve your techniques for solving sudoku puzzles, I recommend that you read my companion volume *How to Solve Sudoku*.

Finally, I'd like to thank my Open University summer school colleagues, especially Alan Slomson, Iain Brodie, Frances Williams and Hilary Short, for finding suitable nine-letter words for inclusion – with special thanks to Richard Copley for computer-generating an extensive list of such words.

Sudoku puzzles can be great fun. Hidden-word puzzles can be even more fun. We hope that after solving the puzzles in this book you will agree.

Robin Wilson

Part 1
Introduction

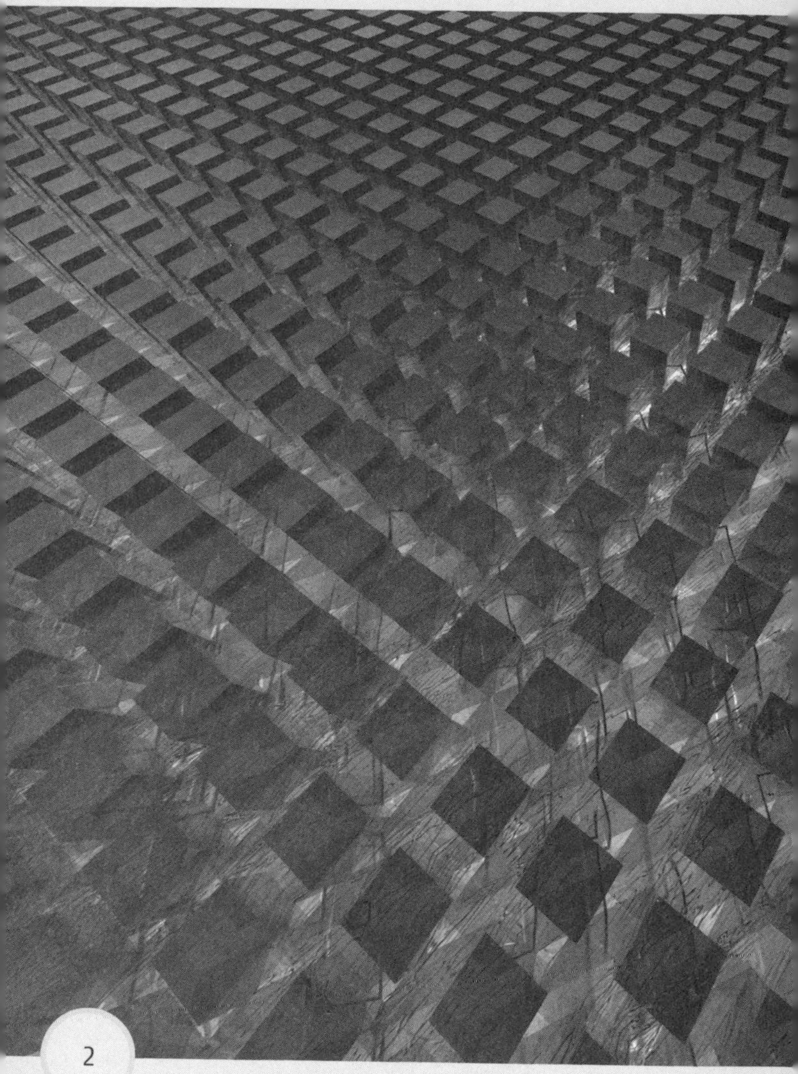

What is sudoku?

A sudoku 'hidden word' puzzle consists of a 9 x 9 grid (nine rows and nine columns), divided into nine 3 x 3 boxes, into which a few letters have already been placed. An example appears overleaf: the nine letters used in the puzzle are listed below the grid.

The object of the puzzle is to fill in all the remaining squares with the given letters, so that each row, each column, and each 3 x 3 box contains all nine letters.

R					W		E	
	W	O			L		D	N
	E		U	R		O		
L				U		N	R	
E			L		F			D
	O	N		E				L
		W		O	E		L	
F	L		R			U	N	
	D		N					W

D E F L N O R U W

Here's the solution to the puzzle opposite.

R	N	F	O	D	W	L	E	U
U	W	O	E	F	L	R	D	N
D	E	L	U	R	N	O	W	F
L	F	D	W	U	O	N	R	E
E	R	U	L	N	F	W	O	D
W	O	N	D	E	R	F	U	L
N	U	W	F	O	E	D	L	R
F	L	E	R	W	D	U	N	O
O	D	R	N	L	U	E	F	W

Notice that each of the nine letters appears just once in each row, once in each column, and once in each 3 x 3 box.

You can also see that the hidden word
WONDERFUL appears in row 6 of the grid.

Hidden words

Each of the puzzles in this book contains a
hidden word that will gradually emerge as you
work through the puzzle.

This hidden word can appear
■ in one of the rows
    – either forward or reversed;
■ in one of the columns
    – either upward or downward;
■ in one of the boxes
    – either horizontally or vertically.

The opposite page shows the various forms in
which the word **WONDERFUL** can appear.

■ rows

W	O	N	D	E	R	F	U	L

L	U	F	R	E	D	N	O	W

<table>
<tr><td>■ columns</td><td>■ boxes</td></tr>
</table>

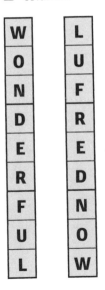

W	O	N
D	E	R
F	U	L

W	D	F
O	E	U
N	R	L

Sudoku techniques: 1

Here we list the basic techniques for solving sudoku puzzles. Further details can be found in the companion book *How to Solve Sudoku*.

There are basically three techniques:

■ scanning the rows and columns for pairs;

R					W		E	
	W	O			L		D	N
	E		U	R		O		
L				U		N	R	
E			L		F			D
	O	N		E				L
		W		O	E		L	
F	L		R			U	N	
	D		N					W

■ filling in the gaps;

■ filling in single cells.

We illustrate these for our earlier puzzle.

Scanning the rows and columns for pairs

Here we choose a block of three rows or three columns: we look for letters that already appear twice and see where the third appearance of that letter might be.

For example, in the top three rows we must put

■ the third R (in row 2) in column 7;

■ the third O (in row 1) in column 4 (there's already an O in column 5);

■ the third W (in row 3) in column 8 (there's already a W in column 9).

Similarly, in the middle three columns we must put

■ the third E (in column 4) in row 2;

■ the third R (in column 6) in row 6;

■ the third U (in column 6) in row 9.

Fill in these letters now and turn over the page.

Sudoku techniques: 2

The grid is now as follows.

R			O		W		E	
	W	O	E		L	R	D	N
	E		U	R		O	W	
L				U		N	R	
E			L		F			D
	O	N		E	R			L
		W		O	E		L	
F	L		R			U	N	
	D		N		U			W

Filling in the gaps

■ In row 2, F and U are missing: we must put U in column 1 and F in column 5.

■ In the top-right box, F, U and L are missing: we must put L in column 7, U in the top-right corner and F in row 3.

Similarly we look for gaps in the other rows, columns and boxes, and fill these in wherever possible.

Filling in single cells

The entry in row 5, column 7 cannot be

■ E, L, F or D (from row 5);

■ R, O, N or U (from column 7);

So it must be W.

Similarly, we consider all the possibilities available for other individual cells and fill these in wherever possible.

Part 2

The puzzles

EASY PUZZLES

1. Food for thought

ACEHKORST

Word: SHORTCAKE

If these puzzles are to your taste, chew them over, digest the information given, and find the hidden delicious morsels.

D G I L M N P S U

Word: _ _ _ _ _ _ _ _ _

2. Heavy weather

N	O	K	A	S	L	E	F	W
W	S	A	N	F	O	K	L	A
L	F	E	W	O	K	N	S	A
K	N	O	S	W	A	L	E	F
A	E	L	O	F	N	K	W	S
F	W	S	K	L	E	A	O	N
O	K	F	L	A	W	S	N	E
E	L	W	N	K	S	F	A	O
S	A	N	F	E	O	W	L	K

A E F K L N O S W

Word: SNOWFLAKE

May the sun shine on you as you storm through
these puzzles like greased lightning, weather or
not you find the hidden words.

A	H	L	S	I	R	O	T	M
R	T	M	L	O	H	S	I	A
I	O	S	A	T	M	R	H	L
L	S	I	R	H	T	A	M	O
T	M	R	O	A	S	H	L	I
O	A	H	M	L	I	T	R	S
M	R	O	T	S	L	I	A	H
H	L	A	I	R	O	M	S	T
S	I	T	H	M	A	L	O	R

A H I L M O R S T

Word: H A I L S T O R M

3. The game's the thing

H	T	L	D	N	O	E	A	C
D	E	C	A	T	H	L	O	N
A	N	O	E	L	C	D	H	T
T	O	N	L	C	A	H	D	E
E	C	H	O	D	T	N	L	A
L	D	A	H	E	N	T		O
C	H	E	T	O	L	A	N	D
O	L	T	N	A	D	C	E	H
N	A	D	C	H	E	O	T	L

A C D E H L N O T

Word: D E C A T H L O N

You don't need to run a marathon to overcome the hurdles involved in finding these hidden terms from the world of sport.

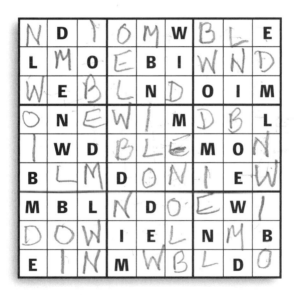

B D E I L M N O W

Word: WLMBLEDON

4. Haughty culture

O	N	F	U	R	S	L	W	E
W	S	R	L	E	F	N	O	U
U	L	E	O	W	N	F	R	S
L	E	N	R	O	U	W	S	F
F	R	O	S	L	W	U	E	N
S	W	U	N	F	E	R	L	O
E	O	L	F	N	R	S	U	W
R	F	S	W	U	O	E	N	L
N	U	W	E	S	L	O	F	R

E F L N O R S U W

Word: S U N F L O W E R

If you're a budding genius (or even a blooming nuisance), you'll be able to locate the hidden words that have been planted here.

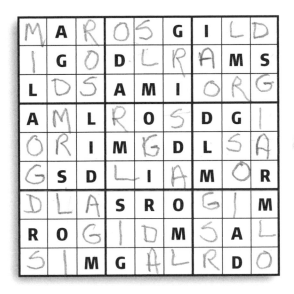

M	A	R	O	S	G	I	L	D
I	G	O	D	L	R	A	M	S
L	D	S	A	M	I	O	R	G
A	M	L	R	O	S	D	G	I
O	R	I	M	G	D	L	S	A
G	S	D	L	I	A	M	O	R
D	L	A	S	R	O	G	I	M
R	O	G	I	D	M	S	A	L
S	I	M	G	A	L	R	D	O

A D G I L M O R S

Word: M A R I G O L D S

5. Home, sweet home

A E F H O M R S U

Word: FARMHOUSE

Don't spend too long dwelling on these residences as you build your techniques for finding the hidden words.

A B G L N O S U W

Word: B U N G A L O W S

6. Around the world

N	I	P	Y	S	E	O	L	A
S	A	O	N	L	I	E	Y	P
Y	E	L	A	O	P	S	I	N
I	P	Y	L	A	O	N	S	E
A	O	N	S	E	Y	I	P	L
L	S	E	I	P	N	Y	A	O
O	Y	S	P	N	A	L	E	I
P	N	I	E	Y	L	A	O	S
E	L	A	O	I	S	P	N	Y

A E I L N O P S Y

Word: POLYNESIA

It won't take you 80 days circumnavigating the globe to find these hidden geographical locations.

A E I G N O P R S

Word: S I N G A P O R E

7. For the birds

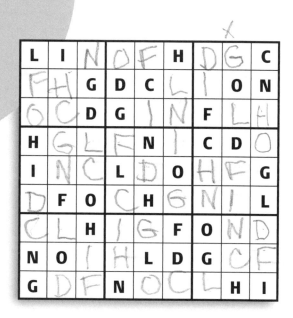

C D F G H I L N O

Word: GOLDFINCH

No larking around! Birds of a feather flock together, but you can find these hidden ornithological words on your own.

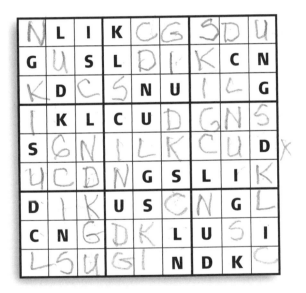

N	L	I	K	C	G	S	D	U
G	U	S	L	D	I	K	C	N
K	D	C	S	N	U	I	L	G
I	K	L	C	U	D	G	N	S
S	G	N	I	L	K	C	U	D
U	C	D	N	G	S	L	I	K
D	I	K	U	S	C	N	G	L
C	N	G	D	K	L	U	S	I
L	S	U	G	I	N	D	K	C

C D I G K L N S U

Word: DUCKLINGS

27

8. All at sea

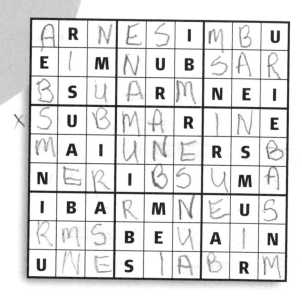

A	R	N	E	S	I	M	B	U
E	I	M	N	U	B	S	A	R
B	S	U	A	R	M	N	E	I
S	U	B	M	A	R	I	N	E
M	A	I	U	N	E	R	S	B
N	E	R	I	B	S	U	M	A
I	B	A	R	M	N	E	U	S
R	M	S	B	E	U	A	I	N
U	N	E	S	I	A	B	R	M

A B E I M N R S U

Word: S U B M A R I N E

28

If you're in the swim of things and can keep your head above water, you'll find these forms of marine craft.

I	S	T	F	L	E	B	A	O
O	A	E	B	T	S	L	F	I
F	L	B	A	O	I	T	E	S
L	I	F	O	E	T	A	S	B
E	B	O	L	S	A	I	T	F
A	T	S	I	B	F	E	O	L
S	O	A	E	I	L	F	B	T
T	E	L	S	F	B	O	I	A
B	F	I	T	A	O	S	L	E

A B E F I L O S T

Word: L I F E B O A T S

MODERATE PUZZLES

9. Animal farm

N	G	O	U	Y	E	H	R	D
Y	R	U	H	D	N	G	O	E
D	E	H	O	G	R	U	Y	N
U	Y	N	D	R	G	E	H	O
G	H	E	N	O	Y	D	U	R
R	O	D	E	H	U	N	G	Y
O	U	R	G	E	D	Y	N	H
E	N	Y	R	U	H	O	D	G
H	D	G	Y	N	O	R	E	U

D E G H N O R U Y

Word: G R E Y H O U N D

Don't think of large animals – they're irr-elephant here. These hidden ones are much smaller.

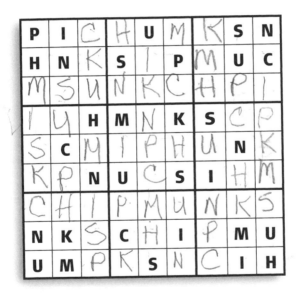

P	I	C	H	U	M	K	S	N
H	N	K	S	I	P	M	U	C
M	S	U	N	K	C	H	P	I
I	U	H	M	N	K	S	C	P
S	C	M	I	P	H	U	N	K
K	P	N	U	C	S	I	H	M
C	H	I	P	M	U	N	K	S
N	K	S	C	H	I	P	M	U
U	M	P	K	S	N	C	I	H

C H I K M N P S U

Word: CHIPMUNKS

10. Rule, Britannia!

B D E G H I N R U

Word: _ _ _ _ _ _ _ _ _

Don't waive the rules as you take a quick trip around Britain in order to locate these famous cities.

		R	C				G	
						A		R
D	M				R			I
	I			A		E		
	C		M		I		R	
		A		G			C	
M			D				B	E
E		D						
	R				A	D		

A B C D E G I M R

Word: _ _ _ _ _ _ _ _ _

11. What do you do, Daddy?

	S						O	
			T		H			
O		H				M		L
	I	T	O		L	S	M	
M								K
	O	S	H			I	L	C
H		K				T		M
			S		M			
	T						L	

C H I K L M O S T

Word: _ _ _ _ _ _ _ _ _

If you occupy your mind you'll be able to do a
good job of finding these hidden occupations.

R			S		H			A
	S	F	A	R	E	N	M	
		R		H		F		
I		H				R		M
		E		F		A		
	R	M	N	A	I	S	H	
A			F		S			E

A E F H I M N R S

Word: _ _ _ _ _ _ _ _ _

12. That figures

S			O				I	
		N					F	
		R	S	I	A			C
	R					I		O
	O		N		T			
C	I					S		
N	T	S	I	C				
	A			N				
	F		A					S

A C F I N O R S T

Word: _ _ _ _ _ _ _ _ _

These are the puzzles that really count – don't become numb-er as you try to figure them out.

Moderate puzzles

		R	M			G	A	
H	G			A	O		L	
O								I
	R							H
	I			G			T	
M							R	
A								G
	O		G	L			I	M
	H	L			M	T		

A G H I L M O R T

Word: _ _ _ _ _ _ _ _ _

13. Oat cuisine

K	R	C					F	
			L	F			K	
		E		A	C			
		N					E	K
C	O					N		
	R	K				O		
	A		F	N				
	E					L	C	N

A C E F K L N O R

Word: _ _ _ _ _ _ _ _ _

Become a cereal killer by demolishing these
a-maize-ing puzzles concerning breakfast foods.

			U				
	U		K		H		T
A	B					K	C
	A	W			T	C	
B		U		A			K
	K	E			W	B	
K	H					A	T
	T		H		K	W	
			E				

A B C E H K T U W

Word: _ _ _ _ _ _ _ _ _

14. Play it again, Sam

						T	I	A
R							E	
N			A		S			L
	C		S		I	L		T
				E				
S		L	T		A		R	
I			C		E			R
	L							S
E	R	N						

A C E I L N R S T

Word: _ _ _ _ _ _ _ _ _

Get in tune with the sounds of these delightful musical instruments – harmony of them are there?

				C				S
	C				E	M		
				R	D	C		
S		L	E					
	D	R	L		U	S	E	
					D	R		C
	E	U	R					
		D	C				S	
L				I				

C D E I L M R S U

Word: _ _ _ _ _ _ _ _ _

41

15. Put it on the map

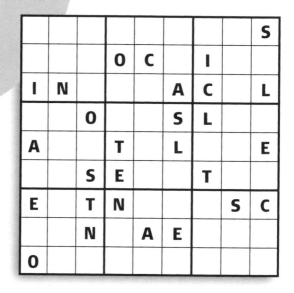

								S
		O	C		I			
I	N				A	C		L
		O			S	L		
A		T			L			E
		S	E			T		
E		T	N				S	C
		N		A	E			
O								

A C E I L N O S T

Word: _ _ _ _ _ _ _ _ _

Study a map for some time, and at-las you should be able to find these hidden geographical terms.

L	I		N		D		U	E
O			E		L			T
				I				
	T	G				E	D	
D								U
	N	L				O	T	
				G				
N			O		T			I
G	U		L		I		E	O

D E G I L N O T U

Word: _ _ _ _ _ _ _ _ _

16. Which way?

		S						H
E			S		R			
Y	L			T				O
	R				L			E
	Y			O			T	
S			H				U	
T				H			S	L
			R		Y			U
H						O		

E H L O R S T U Y

Word: _ _ _ _ _ _ _ _ _

Losing your direction? These hidden words should help to put you back on the right track.

	E	W	N					
			W					N
		O	U	S		T		W
						D		B
	U	T				W	O	
W		N						
B		U		E	S	O		
E				U				
					O	U	B	

B D E N O S T U W

Word: _ _ _ _ _ _ _ _ _

HARD PUZZLES

17. House proud

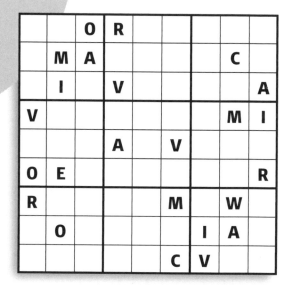

		O	R					
	M	A					C	
	I		V					A
V						M	I	
		A		V				
O	E							R
R				M		W		
	O					I	A	
				C	V			

A C E I M O R V W

Word: _ _ _ _ _ _ _ _ _

You'll find these hidden words as you go around the house – move your hand slightly for the first one.

				S	O	D		
P	S						O	
			B					
U		C						R
R	A				O			D
D				B				U
			O					
	O						A	B
		R	D	U				

A B C D O P R S U

Word: _ _ _ _ _ _ _ _ _

18. The world of science

	T				P			C
			N	U				
	I					P	G	
			U				C	
	P	T				M	N	
	U				O			
	G	N					O	
				O	M			
T			I				M	

C G I M N O P T U

Word: _ _ _ _ _ _ _ _ _

There are many wonderful branches of science – here are two very different ones.

E	R							S
	I			C				
		T				E	H	R
		E	R					Y
			I	S	M			
R					C	T		
M	T	R				S		
				I			E	
S							M	C

C E H I M R S T Y

Word: _ _ _ _ _ _ _ _ _

19. Staying stationery

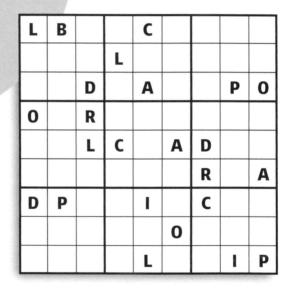

				C				
L	B			C				
			L					
		D		A			P	O
O		R						
		L	C		A	D		
					R			A
D	P			I		C		
					O			
				L			I	P

A B C D I L O P R

Word: _ _ _ _ _ _ _ _ _

Paper over the cracks as you locate these useful items from the stationer's shop.

		H	T					
			S	C	A			H
	T					K	S	
C	P							
			S	H	T			
							D	K
H	S					P		
E		A	H	P				
				A	S			

A C D E H K P S T

Word: _ _ _ _ _ _ _ _ _

51

20. Follow my leader

	B		H		R		V	
		A		O		E		
			C		B			
O				V				E
		E				O		
A				G				V
			B		O			
		V		R		G		
	C		V		G		E	

A B C E G H O R V

Word: _ _ _ _ _ _ _ _ _

Past and present political leaders from around the world are De Gaulle of this puzzle – in case you Adenauer to spare.

A	N	L					T	
			Y				B	
					N			
O			R		B		L	
		N				O		
	I		A		Y			T
		O						
	T				I			
	Y					T	A	O

A B I L N O R T Y

Word: _ _ _ _ _ _ _ _ _

21. Paperback writer

I	G		W			N		
			R				J	I
O			I				W	
						R	K	
			O	J	I			
	N	L						
	K				N			W
L	O				W			
		G			O		L	N

G I J K L N O R W

Word: _ _ _ _ _ _ _ _ _

Don't get writer's cramp solving these novel
puzzles – the authors provide the hidden words.

M			E	I	W			A
A	Y						W	M
		N	H		A	G		
E								N
		Y	N		E	A		
W	N						I	G
Y			A	W	M			E

A E G H I M N W Y

Word: _ _ _ _ _ _ _ _ _

22. Eastern Europe

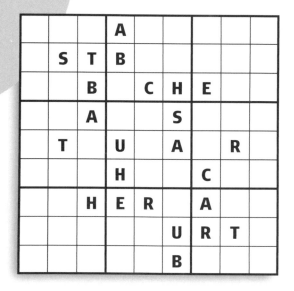

A B C E H R S T U

Word: _ _ _ _ _ _ _ _ _

Hungary for more puzzles? Find these Eastern
European cities and then Czech your answers.

	V			N	B			
								D
		R		K	U	V		
N		K						
O		B		V		R		N
						D		B
		D	R	B		O		
R								
			O	I			B	

B D I K N O R U V

Word: _ _ _ _ _ _ _ _ _

23. Just for the halibut

C			R	H	S			
			A			H		
							R	
L			H	I		D		
	P						S	
		D	L	C				R
	I							
		H		P				
		A	R	D				P

A C D H I L P R S

Word: _ _ _ _ _ _ _ _ _

Plaice the letters correctly and solve these fishy puzzles – good for the sole!

		I	V				N	O
		S	A		H			
	H			C	O		S	
I								V
O	N	E			A			
	V		I	S				
S	C				H	E		

A C E H I N O S V

Word: _ _ _ _ _ _ _ _ _

24. Body language

H			M		U			B
	U			B			H	
		A		L		I		
A			N		B			L
B			U		A			T
		T		U		M		
	M			N			I	
U			T		I			H

A B H I L M N T U

Word: _ _ _ _ _ _ _ _ _

Every-body should have these – the first one should easily come to hand.

N						I	M	G
			A	E	S			
M				I	T	G		
	S					L		
	I	E	G					N
	G	N	T					
E	A	M						S

A E G I L M N S T

Word: _ _ _ _ _ _ _ _ _

FIENDISH PUZZLES
25. It's the law

	S	E						B
	B	T	C				N	
					L			
				E	T	B		
		L		B				
	C	L	O					
	N							
	E				O	A	C	
A						N	T	

A B C E L N O S T

Word: _ _ _ _ _ _ _ _ _

It's a fair cop! You'll be captivated by these puzzles and should be able to solve them with conviction.

	O		N		C		E	
		I		E		C		
			L					
M	C						A	I
A								N
E	I						L	C
			M					
		A		N		P		
	E		L		I		N	

A C E I L M N O P

Word: _ _ _ _ _ _ _ _ _

26. I've got a little list

M								D
D	K	E				T		A
	A		M					
T					E	H		
			H		O			
		I	D					M
				K		D		
O		H				K	A	T
A								I

A D E H I K M O T

Word: _ _ _ _ _ _ _ _ _

Enter the delightful world of comic opera by
solving these puzzles – they may need some
Patience.

				S				
		I			W	R		
	G	W				B	T	
	I		L		T			
T				E				R
			W			I		E
	B	L					S	W
		R	G				I	
				L				

B E G I L R S T W

Word: _ _ _ _ _ _ _ _ _ _

27. Back to school

	T		A					I
U		E	T					
		A		C				
C				I				
	N			E			O	
				O				A
				D		A		
					U	T		D
N						E		

A C D E I N O T U

Word: _ _ _ _ _ _ _ _ _

These puzzles may revive happy memories of your schooldays and of the styles of teaching you received there.

	C	G			R			E
	I	N	C					
							T	
			C	N	T	L		
		T		U				
	U	T	I	R				
	N							
				G	N	U		
R			L			G	I	

C E G I L N R T U

Word: _ _ _ _ _ _ _ _ _

28. Fizz with physics

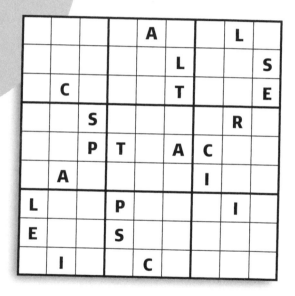

A C E I L P R S T

Word: _ _ _ _ _ _ _ _ _

Enter the fascinating world of small-scale physics and find these related hidden words.

B	C	A			M			
			T					O
	I							C
		O		U			A	
		C				M		
	A			I		U		
M							T	
C					S			
		B				I	C	S

A B C I M O S T U

Word: _ _ _ _ _ _ _ _ _

29. Singing in the Rhine

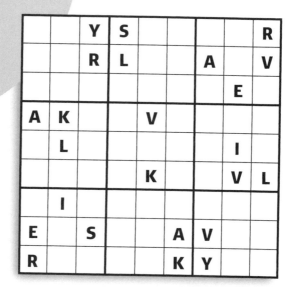

		Y	S					R
		R	L			A		V
							E	
A	K			V				
	L						I	
			K				V	L
	I							
E		S			A	V		
R					K	Y		

A E I K L R S V Y

Word: _ _ _ _ _ _ _ _ _

These puzzles take you into the world of Wagner – hopefully your solutions will Ring true.

				L	O		E	
O								
		N	D			L		
L			R		G	H		
E								I
		R	O		N			D
		H		L	G			
								R
	D		H	N				

D E G H I L N O R

Word: _ _ _ _ _ _ _ _ _

30. Pantomime season

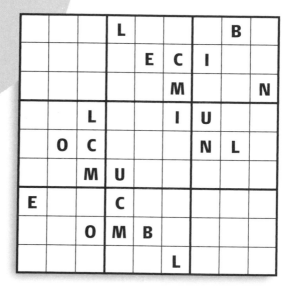

B C E I L M N O U

Word: _ _ _ _ _ _ _ _ _

No Aladdins or Cinderellas here – these related puzzles transport you back to traditional pantomime.

	Q	I	L	U	E			
U				I			H	
Q		R		H		A		
	U						E	
		E		N		Q		R
	A			R				N
			N	A	U	I	Q	

A E H I L N Q R U

Word: _ _ _ _ _ _ _ _ _

31. Getting technical

V	I		R		Y		G	U
G				I				R
	N						I	
			E		S			
U								N
			V		N			
	E						U	
Y				S				G
R	U		I		E		N	S

E G I N R S U V Y

Word: _ _ _ _ _ _ _ _ _

Enroll at a technical college if you wish to study these subjects – or find them by solving the puzzles.

W	A				R		L	
							E	
			E	K	R			
	O			W				
E				R				T
			A				M	
	K	T	A					
	L							
	M		L				A	O

A E K L M O R T W

Word: _ _ _ _ _ _ _ _ _

32. Relax with a drink

C			N					
E			R	U		I		
			O		I			N
		E				A		
		R				C		
		I				O		
U			E		O			
		A		R	U			T
					A			R

A C E I N O R T U

Word: _ _ _ _ _ _ _ _ _

After solving all these puzzles you deserve a break with your favorite beverage.

	O	I	N	A	T			
T				E			A	
E		O		T		L		
	L						N	
		A		F		E		O
	F			I				N
			L	N	P	I	O	

A E F I L N O P T

Word: _ _ _ _ _ _ _ _ _

Part 3

Solutions

1. Food for thought

E	R	H	O	S	A	K	C	T
C	T	K	H	E	R	S	O	A
A	O	S	C	K	T	R	E	H
K	C	R	A	O	E	T	H	S
S	H	O	R	T	C	A	K	E
T	E	A	K	H	S	O	R	C
R	A	T	E	C	K	H	S	O
O	S	C	T	R	H	E	A	K
H	K	E	S	A	O	C	T	R

Word: **SHORTCAKE**

L	D	I	S	P	G	N	M	U
S	U	P	M	L	N	I	G	D
G	M	N	U	I	D	L	P	S
U	P	G	D	S	I	M	N	L
M	L	S	N	U	P	G	D	I
N	I	D	G	M	L	S	U	P
P	N	L	I	D	M	U	S	G
D	G	U	L	N	S	P	I	M
I	S	M	P	G	U	D	L	N

Word: **DUMPLINGS**

2. Heavy weather

N	O	K	A	S	L	E	F	W
W	S	A	E	N	F	O	K	L
L	F	E	W	O	K	N	S	A
K	N	O	S	W	A	L	E	F
A	E	L	O	F	N	K	W	S
F	W	S	K	L	E	A	O	N
O	K	F	L	A	W	S	N	E
E	L	W	N	K	S	F	A	O
S	A	N	F	E	O	W	L	K

Word: **S N O W F L A K E**

A	H	L	S	I	R	O	T	M
R	T	M	L	O	H	S	I	A
I	O	S	A	T	M	R	H	L
L	S	I	R	H	T	A	M	O
T	M	R	O	A	S	H	L	I
O	A	H	M	L	I	T	R	S
M	R	O	T	S	L	I	A	H
H	L	A	I	R	O	M	S	T
S	I	T	H	M	A	L	O	R

Word: **H A I L S T O R M**

81

3. The game's the thing

H	T	L	D	N	O	E	A	C
D	E	C	A	T	H	L	O	N
A	N	O	E	L	C	D	H	T
T	O	N	L	C	A	H	D	E
E	C	H	O	D	T	N	L	A
L	D	A	H	E	N	T	C	O
C	H	E	T	O	L	A	N	D
O	L	T	N	A	D	C	E	H
N	A	D	C	H	E	O	T	L

Word: **DECATHLON**

N	D	I	O	M	W	B	L	E
L	M	O	E	B	I	W	N	D
W	E	B	L	N	D	O	I	M
O	N	E	W	I	M	D	B	L
I	W	D	B	L	E	M	O	N
B	L	M	D	O	N	I	E	W
M	B	L	N	D	O	E	W	I
D	O	W	I	E	L	N	M	B
E	I	N	M	W	B	L	D	O

Word: **WIMBLEDON**

4. Haughty culture

O	N	F	U	R	S	L	W	E
W	S	R	L	E	F	N	O	U
U	L	E	O	W	N	F	R	S
L	E	N	R	O	U	W	S	F
F	R	O	S	L	W	U	E	N
S	W	U	N	F	E	R	L	O
E	O	L	F	N	R	S	U	W
R	F	S	W	U	O	E	N	L
N	U	W	E	S	L	O	F	R

Word: **S U N F L O W E R**

M	A	R	O	S	G	I	L	D
I	G	O	D	L	R	A	M	S
L	D	S	A	M	I	O	R	G
A	M	L	R	O	S	D	G	I
O	R	I	M	G	D	L	S	A
G	S	D	L	I	A	M	O	R
D	L	A	S	R	O	G	I	M
R	O	G	I	D	M	S	A	L
S	I	M	G	A	L	R	D	O

Word: **M A R I G O L D S**

5. Home, sweet home

H	E	O	F	A	U	M	R	S
U	M	A	O	R	S	F	E	H
R	F	S	H	E	M	O	A	U
E	S	H	A	U	F	R	O	M
F	A	R	M	H	O	U	S	E
M	O	U	E	S	R	A	H	F
O	R	F	S	M	E	H	U	A
S	H	M	U	O	A	E	F	R
A	U	E	R	F	H	S	M	O

Word: **FARMHOUSE**

U	L	A	W	B	O	N	S	G
G	S	O	N	A	L	B	W	U
W	B	N	S	G	U	A	O	L
B	U	W	G	O	A	S	L	N
O	N	G	B	L	S	U	A	W
S	A	L	U	N	W	O	G	B
L	G	S	O	U	B	W	N	A
A	O	B	L	W	N	G	U	S
N	W	U	A	S	G	L	B	O

Word: **BUNGALOWS**

6. Around the world

N	I	P	Y	S	E	O	L	A
S	A	O	N	L	I	E	Y	P
Y	E	L	A	O	P	S	I	N
I	P	Y	L	A	O	N	S	E
A	O	N	S	E	Y	I	P	L
L	S	E	I	P	N	Y	A	O
O	Y	S	P	N	A	L	E	I
P	N	I	E	Y	L	A	O	S
E	L	A	O	I	S	P	N	Y

Word: **P O L Y N E S I A**

R	N	E	A	P	I	S	G	O
P	G	S	O	N	E	I	A	R
O	I	A	R	G	S	N	P	E
N	P	O	G	I	A	E	R	S
E	S	R	N	O	P	A	I	G
G	A	I	E	S	R	O	N	P
I	O	P	S	A	G	R	E	N
A	R	N	P	E	O	G	S	I
S	E	G	I	R	N	P	O	A

Word: **S I N G A P O R E**

7. For the birds

L	I	N	O	F	H	D	G	C
F	H	G	D	C	L	I	O	N
O	C	D	G	I	N	F	L	H
H	G	L	F	N	I	C	D	O
I	N	C	L	D	O	H	F	G
D	F	O	C	H	G	N	I	L
C	L	H	I	G	F	O	N	D
N	O	I	H	L	D	G	C	F
G	D	F	N	O	C	L	H	I

Word: **GOLDFINCH**

N	L	I	K	C	G	S	D	U
G	U	S	L	D	I	K	C	N
K	D	C	S	N	U	I	L	G
I	K	L	C	U	D	G	N	S
S	G	N	I	L	K	C	U	D
U	C	D	N	G	S	L	I	K
D	I	K	U	S	C	N	G	L
C	N	G	D	K	L	U	S	I
L	S	U	G	I	N	D	K	C

Word: **DUCKLINGS**

8. All at sea

A	R	N	E	S	I	M	B	U
E	I	M	N	U	B	S	A	R
B	S	U	A	R	M	N	E	I
S	**U**	**B**	**M**	**A**	**R**	**I**	**N**	**E**
M	A	I	U	N	E	R	S	B
N	E	R	I	B	S	U	M	A
I	B	A	R	M	N	E	U	S
R	M	S	B	E	U	A	I	N
U	N	E	S	I	A	B	R	M

Word: **SUBMARINE**

I	S	T	F	L	E	B	A	O
O	A	E	B	T	S	L	F	I
F	L	B	A	O	I	T	E	S
L	**I**	**F**	O	E	T	A	S	B
E	**B**	**O**	L	S	A	I	T	F
A	T	**S**	I	B	F	E	O	L
S	O	A	E	I	L	F	B	T
T	E	L	S	F	B	O	I	A
B	F	I	T	A	O	S	L	E

Word: **LIFEBOATS**

87

9. Animal farm

N	G	O	U	Y	E	H	R	D
Y	R	U	H	D	N	G	O	E
D	E	H	O	G	R	U	Y	N
U	Y	N	D	R	G	E	H	O
G	H	E	N	O	Y	D	U	R
R	O	D	E	H	U	N	G	Y
O	U	R	G	E	D	Y	N	H
E	N	Y	R	U	H	O	D	G
H	D	G	Y	N	O	R	E	U

Word: **GREYHOUND**

P	I	C	H	U	M	K	S	N
H	N	K	S	I	P	M	U	C
M	S	U	N	K	C	H	P	I
I	U	H	M	N	K	S	C	P
S	C	M	I	P	H	U	N	K
K	P	N	U	C	S	I	H	M
C	H	I	P	M	U	N	K	S
N	K	S	C	H	I	P	M	U
U	M	P	K	S	N	C	I	H

Word: **CHIPMUNKS**

10. Rule, Britannia!

U	I	N	H	E	B	D	R	G
E	B	G	D	U	R	N	H	I
D	R	H	G	I	N	B	E	U
H	N	U	E	D	I	R	G	B
G	E	R	N	B	U	H	I	D
I	D	B	R	G	H	E	U	N
N	H	I	B	R	G	U	D	E
B	G	D	U	H	E	I	N	R
R	U	E	I	N	D	G	B	H

Word: **EDINBURGH**

A	E	R	C	I	M	B	G	D
I	B	C	G	E	D	A	M	R
D	M	G	A	B	R	C	E	I
G	I	M	R	A	C	E	D	B
B	C	E	M	D	I	G	R	A
R	D	A	B	G	E	I	C	M
M	A	I	D	C	G	R	B	E
E	G	D	I	R	B	M	A	C
C	R	B	E	M	A	D	I	G

Word: **CAMBRIDGE**

11. What do you do, Daddy?

T	S	C	M	L	K	H	O	I
L	M	I	T	O	H	C	K	S
O	K	H	I	C	S	M	T	L
C	I	T	O	K	L	S	M	H
M	H	L	C	S	T	O	I	K
K	O	S	H	M	I	L	C	T
H	C	K	L	I	O	T	S	M
I	L	O	S	T	M	K	H	C
S	T	M	K	H	C	I	L	O

Word: **L O C K S M I T H**

N	E	A	M	I	F	H	S	R
R	M	I	S	N	H	E	F	A
H	S	F	A	R	E	N	M	I
M	A	R	I	H	N	F	E	S
I	F	H	E	S	A	R	N	M
S	N	E	R	F	M	A	I	H
E	R	M	N	A	I	S	H	F
A	H	N	F	M	S	I	R	E
F	I	S	H	E	R	M	A	N

Word: **F I S H E R M A N**

12. That figures

S	C	A	F	O	T	R	I	N
O	I	R	N	C	A	S	F	T
T	N	F	R	S	I	A	O	C
F	R	N	C	T	S	I	A	O
A	S	O	I	N	F	T	C	R
C	T	I	A	R	O	N	S	F
N	O	T	S	I	C	F	R	A
R	A	S	O	F	N	C	T	I
I	F	C	T	A	R	O	N	S

Word: **FRACTIONS**

I	T	R	M	H	L	G	A	O
H	G	M	I	A	O	R	L	T
O	L	A	T	R	G	H	M	I
T	R	O	L	M	A	I	G	H
L	I	H	O	G	R	M	T	A
M	A	G	H	T	I	O	R	L
A	M	I	R	O	T	L	H	G
R	O	T	G	L	H	A	I	M
G	H	L	A	I	M	T	O	R

Word: **LOGARITHM**

13. Oat cuisine

K	R	C	N	O	E	A	F	L
A	N	O	C	L	F	E	K	R
L	F	E	R	K	A	C	N	O
R	L	N	A	C	O	F	E	K
E	K	A	L	F	N	R	O	C
C	O	F	E	R	K	N	L	A
N	C	R	K	E	L	O	A	F
O	A	L	F	N	C	K	R	E
F	E	K	O	A	R	L	C	N

Word: **C O R N F L A K E**

T	E	K	A	U	C	B	H	W
W	U	C	K	B	H	A	T	E
A	B	H	E	T	W	U	K	C
H	A	W	B	K	E	T	C	U
B	C	T	U	W	A	H	E	K
U	K	E	C	H	T	W	B	A
K	H	B	W	C	U	E	A	T
E	T	U	H	A	K	C	W	B
C	W	A	T	E	B	K	U	H

Word: **B U C K W H E A T**

14. Play it again, Sam

L	S	C	E	N	R	T	I	A
R	A	T	I	L	C	S	E	N
N	E	I	A	T	S	R	C	L
A	C	E	S	R	I	L	N	T
T	I	R	N	E	L	A	S	C
S	N	L	T	C	A	I	R	E
I	T	S	C	A	E	N	L	R
C	**L**	**A**	**R**	**I**	**N**	**E**	**T**	**S**
E	R	N	L	S	T	C	A	I

Word: **CLARINETS**

D	R	E	M	C	I	L	U	**S**
U	C	S	D	L	E	M	I	**R**
M	L	I	S	U	R	D	C	**E**
S	I	L	E	R	C	U	D	**M**
C	D	R	L	M	U	S	E	**I**
E	U	M	I	S	D	R	L	**C**
I	E	U	R	D	S	C	M	**L**
R	M	D	C	E	L	I	S	**U**
L	S	C	U	I	M	E	R	**D**

Word: **DULCIMERS**

15. Put it on the map

C	O	A	L	E	I	N	T	S
S	T	L	O	C	N	I	E	A
I	N	E	S	T	A	C	O	L
T	E	O	A	N	S	L	C	I
A	C	I	T	O	L	S	N	E
N	L	S	E	I	C	T	A	O
E	I	T	N	L	O	A	S	C
L	S	N	C	A	E	O	I	T
O	A	C	I	S	T	E	L	N

Word: **COASTLINE**

L	I	T	N	O	D	G	U	E
O	G	N	E	U	L	D	I	T
E	D	U	T	I	G	N	O	L
U	T	G	I	L	O	E	D	U
D	E	O	G	T	N	I	L	U
I	N	L	D	E	U	O	T	G
T	O	I	U	G	E	L	N	D
N	L	E	O	D	T	U	G	I
G	U	D	L	N	I	T	E	O

Word: **LONGITUDE**

16. Which way?

R	T	S	L	U	O	E	Y	H
E	H	O	S	Y	R	U	L	T
Y	L	U	E	T	H	S	R	O
U	R	T	Y	S	L	H	O	E
L	Y	H	U	O	E	R	T	S
S	O	E	H	R	T	L	U	Y
T	E	R	O	H	U	Y	S	L
O	S	L	R	E	Y	T	H	U
H	U	Y	T	L	S	O	E	R

Word: **S O U T H E R L Y**

S	E	W	N	D	T	B	U	O
U	T	B	O	W	E	S	D	N
N	D	O	U	S	B	T	E	W
O	S	E	W	T	U	D	N	B
D	U	T	E	B	N	W	O	S
W	B	N	S	O	D	E	T	U
B	N	U	T	E	S	O	W	D
E	O	D	B	U	W	N	S	T
T	W	S	D	N	O	U	B	E

Word: **W E S T B O U N D**

17. Home, sweet home

C	V	O	R	M	A	W	I	E
W	M	A	E	I	O	R	C	V
E	I	R	V	C	W	M	O	A
V	A	W	C	R	E	O	M	I
I	R	M	A	O	V	C	E	W
O	E	C	M	W	I	A	V	R
R	C	V	I	A	M	E	W	O
M	O	E	W	V	R	I	A	C
A	W	I	O	E	C	V	R	M

Word: **MICROWAVE**

A	R	B	P	S	O	D	U	C
P	S	C	U	D	R	B	O	A
O	D	U	A	B	C	S	R	P
U	B	O	C	A	D	P	S	R
R	C	A	S	P	U	O	B	D
D	P	S	O	R	B	A	C	U
C	U	P	B	O	A	R	D	S
S	O	D	R	C	P	U	A	B
B	A	R	D	U	S	C	P	O

Word: **CUPBOARDS**

18. The world of science

G	T	O	M	I	P	N	U	C
P	M	C	N	U	G	I	T	O
N	I	U	O	T	C	P	G	M
I	N	G	U	M	T	O	C	P
O	P	T	C	G	I	M	N	U
C	U	M	P	N	O	G	I	T
M	G	N	T	P	U	C	O	I
U	C	I	G	O	M	T	P	N
T	O	P	I	C	N	U	M	G

Word: **COMPUTING**

E	R	Y	H	M	T	I	C	S
H	I	S	E	C	R	Y	T	M
C	M	T	S	Y	I	E	H	R
I	C	E	R	T	H	M	S	Y
T	Y	H	I	S	M	C	R	E
R	S	M	Y	E	C	T	I	H
M	T	R	C	H	E	S	Y	I
Y	H	C	M	I	S	R	E	T
S	E	I	T	R	Y	H	M	C

Word: **CHEMISTRY**

19. Staying stationery

L	B	P	O	C	D	I	A	R
R	O	A	L	P	I	B	D	C
I	C	D	R	A	B	L	P	O
O	A	R	B	D	L	P	C	I
P	I	L	C	R	A	D	O	B
B	D	C	I	O	P	R	L	A
D	P	O	A	I	R	C	B	L
C	L	I	P	B	O	A	R	D
A	R	B	D	L	C	O	I	P

Word: **C L I P B O A R D**

S	A	H	T	K	P	D	E	C
P	K	E	D	S	C	A	T	H
D	T	C	E	A	H	P	K	S
C	P	T	A	D	K	H	S	E
K	E	D	S	H	T	C	A	P
A	H	S	P	C	E	T	D	K
H	S	K	C	T	D	E	P	A
E	D	A	H	P	S	K	C	T
T	C	P	K	E	A	S	H	D

Word: **S K E T C H P A D**

20. Follow my leader

G	B	O	H	E	R	C	V	A
C	R	A	G	O	V	E	B	H
V	E	H	C	A	B	R	O	G
O	G	B	R	V	C	H	A	E
R	V	E	A	B	H	O	G	C
A	H	C	O	G	E	B	R	V
E	A	G	B	C	O	V	H	R
H	O	V	E	R	A	G	C	B
B	C	R	V	H	G	A	E	O

Word: **GORBACHEV**

A	N	L	B	I	O	Y	T	R
T	O	I	Y	R	N	A	B	L
B	R	Y	L	A	T	N	O	I
O	A	T	R	N	B	I	L	Y
Y	B	N	I	T	L	O	R	A
L	I	R	A	O	Y	B	N	T
N	L	O	T	Y	A	R	I	B
R	T	A	O	B	I	L	Y	N
I	Y	B	N	L	R	T	A	O

Word: **TONY BLAIR**

21. Paperback writer

I	G	J	W	O	K	N	R	L
N	W	K	R	L	G	O	J	I
O	L	R	I	N	J	G	W	K
G	I	O	N	W	L	R	K	J
K	R	W	O	J	I	L	N	G
J	N	L	G	K	R	W	I	O
R	K	I	L	G	N	J	O	W
L	O	N	J	I	W	K	G	R
W	J	G	K	R	O	I	L	N

Word: **JK ROWLING**

M	H	G	E	I	W	N	Y	A
N	I	W	M	A	Y	E	G	H
A	Y	E	G	H	N	I	W	M
I	M	N	H	Y	A	G	E	W
E	A	H	W	G	I	Y	M	N
G	W	Y	N	M	E	A	H	I
W	N	A	Y	E	H	M	I	G
H	E	M	I	N	G	W	A	Y
Y	G	I	A	W	M	H	N	E

Word: **HEMINGWAY**

22. Eastern Europe

E	H	R	A	S	T	B	U	C
C	S	T	B	U	E	H	A	R
U	A	B	R	C	H	E	S	T
R	E	A	C	B	S	T	H	U
H	T	C	U	E	A	S	R	B
S	B	U	H	T	R	C	E	A
T	U	H	E	R	C	A	B	S
B	C	E	S	A	U	R	T	H
A	R	S	T	H	B	U	C	E

Word: **BUCHAREST**

D	V	U	I	N	B	K	R	O
K	I	N	V	O	R	B	U	D
B	O	R	D	K	U	V	N	I
N	R	K	B	D	O	U	I	V
O	D	B	U	V	I	R	K	N
V	U	I	K	R	N	D	O	B
I	N	D	R	B	K	O	V	U
R	B	O	N	U	V	I	D	K
U	K	V	O	I	D	N	B	R

Word: **DUBROVNIK**

23. Just for the halibut

C	D	P	L	R	H	S	A	I
R	L	S	A	P	I	H	C	D
A	H	I	S	C	D	P	R	L
L	A	R	H	I	S	D	P	C
I	P	C	D	A	R	L	S	H
H	S	D	P	L	C	A	I	R
P	I	L	C	H	A	R	D	S
D	R	H	I	S	P	C	L	A
S	C	A	R	D	L	I	H	P

Word: **PILCHARDS**

A	H	I	V	C	E	S	N	O
N	O	E	S	A	I	H	V	C
C	V	S	H	O	N	I	A	E
V	A	H	I	N	C	O	E	S
I	E	C	O	S	A	N	H	V
O	S	N	E	H	V	A	C	I
H	I	A	C	E	O	V	S	N
E	N	V	A	I	S	C	O	H
S	C	O	N	V	H	E	I	A

Word: **ANCHOVIES**

24. Body language

H	N	I	M	A	U	L	T	B
M	U	L	I	B	T	N	H	A
T	B	A	H	L	N	I	U	M
A	I	H	N	T	B	U	M	L
N	T	U	L	H	M	A	B	I
B	L	M	U	I	A	H	N	T
I	H	T	B	U	L	M	A	N
L	M	B	A	N	H	T	I	U
U	A	N	T	M	I	B	L	H

Word: **T H U M B N A I L**

T	M	S	I	G	N	L	A	E
N	E	A	T	S	L	I	M	G
L	G	I	M	A	E	S	N	T
M	N	L	S	E	I	T	G	A
G	S	T	A	N	M	E	L	I
A	I	E	G	L	T	M	S	N
I	L	G	N	T	S	A	E	M
E	A	M	L	I	G	N	T	S
S	T	N	E	M	A	G	I	L

Word: **L I G A M E N T S**

25. It's the law

L	S	E	T	A	N	C	O	B
O	B	T	C	E	L	S	N	A
N	A	C	B	O	S	L	E	T
S	N	O	A	C	E	T	B	L
E	T	A	L	N	B	O	S	C
B	C	L	O	S	T	E	A	N
C	O	N	S	T	A	B	L	E
T	E	B	N	L	O	A	C	S
A	L	S	E	B	C	N	T	O

Word: **CONSTABLE**

P	O	M	N	I	C	L	E	A
L	N	I	A	E	P	C	M	O
C	A	E	O	L	M	N	I	P
M	C	N	P	O	L	E	A	I
A	L	O	I	C	E	M	P	N
E	I	P	M	A	N	O	L	C
N	P	L	C	M	A	I	O	E
I	M	A	E	N	O	P	C	L
O	E	C	L	P	I	A	N	M

Word: **POLICEMAN**

26. I've got a little list

M	I	O	K	T	A	E	H	D
D	K	E	O	H	I	T	M	A
H	A	T	M	E	D	I	K	O
T	O	D	A	M	E	H	I	K
K	M	A	H	I	O	D	T	E
E	H	I	D	K	T	A	O	M
I	T	M	E	A	K	O	D	H
O	E	H	I	D	M	K	A	T
A	D	K	T	O	H	M	E	I

Word: **THE MIKADO**

L	R	T	B	S	E	W	G	I
B	E	I	T	G	W	R	L	S
S	G	W	R	I	L	B	T	E
R	I	E	L	B	T	G	S	W
T	W	B	S	E	G	L	I	R
G	L	S	W	R	I	T	E	B
I	B	L	E	T	R	S	W	G
E	T	R	G	W	S	I	B	L
W	S	G	I	L	B	E	R	T

Word: **WS GILBERT**

27. Back to school

D	T	N	A	U	O	E	C	I
U	C	E	T	N	I	D	A	O
O	I	A	D	C	E	U	T	N
C	O	T	U	I	A	N	D	E
A	N	U	C	E	D	I	O	T
E	D	I	N	O	T	C	U	A
T	U	O	E	D	N	A	I	C
I	E	C	O	A	U	T	N	D
N	A	D	I	T	C	O	E	U

Word: **E D U C A T I O N**

T	C	G	U	L	R	I	N	E
U	I	N	C	T	E	L	R	G
E	L	R	N	G	I	U	T	C
I	R	E	G	C	N	T	L	U
N	G	L	T	E	U	R	C	I
C	U	T	I	R	L	E	G	N
G	N	I	R	U	T	C	E	L
L	T	C	E	I	G	N	U	R
R	E	U	L	N	C	G	I	T

Word: **L E C T U R I N G**

28. Fizz with physics

P	S	E	R	A	C	T	L	I
A	T	I	E	P	L	R	C	S
R	C	L	I	S	T	P	A	E
T	L	S	C	I	P	E	R	A
I	E	P	T	R	A	C	S	L
C	A	R	L	E	S	I	P	T
L	R	A	P	T	E	S	I	C
E	P	C	S	L	I	A	T	R
S	I	T	A	C	R	L	E	P

Word: **PARTICLES**

B	C	A	O	S	M	T	I	U
S	U	M	T	C	I	A	B	O
O	I	T	U	B	A	S	M	C
I	M	O	S	U	B	C	A	T
U	B	C	A	T	O	M	S	I
T	A	S	M	I	C	U	O	B
M	S	I	C	O	U	B	T	A
C	T	B	I	A	S	O	U	M
A	O	U	B	M	T	I	C	S

Word: **SUBATOMIC**

29. Singing in the Rhine

I	E	Y	S	A	V	L	K	R
K	S	R	L	E	I	A	Y	V
V	A	L	K	Y	R	I	E	S
A	K	E	I	V	L	S	R	Y
S	L	V	Y	R	E	K	I	A
Y	R	I	A	K	S	E	V	L
L	I	K	V	S	Y	R	A	E
E	Y	S	R	I	A	V	L	K
R	V	A	E	L	K	Y	S	I

Word: **VALKYRIES**

D	R	G	N	L	O	I	E	H
O	H	L	E	R	I	N	D	G
I	E	N	D	G	H	L	R	O
L	I	D	R	E	G	H	O	N
E	N	O	L	H	D	R	G	I
H	G	R	O	I	N	E	L	D
R	O	H	I	D	L	G	N	E
N	L	I	G	O	E	D	H	R
G	D	E	H	N	R	O	I	L

Word: **RHEINGOLD**

30. Pantomime season

C	U	I	L	N	O	E	B	M
O	M	N	B	E	C	I	U	L
L	B	E	I	U	M	O	C	N
B	N	L	O	C	I	U	M	E
U	O	C	E	M	B	N	L	I
I	E	M	U	L	N	C	O	B
E	L	B	C	I	U	M	N	O
N	C	O	M	B	E	L	I	U
M	I	U	N	O	L	B	E	C

Word: **COLUMBINE**

R	E	A	H	Q	N	U	I	L
H	Q	I	L	U	E	N	R	A
U	N	L	A	I	R	E	H	Q
Q	L	R	E	H	I	A	N	U
A	U	N	R	L	Q	H	E	I
I	H	E	U	N	A	Q	L	R
E	A	Q	I	R	H	L	U	N
L	R	H	N	A	U	I	Q	E
N	I	U	Q	E	L	R	A	H

Word: **HARLEQUIN**

31. Getting technical

V	I	S	R	E	Y	N	G	U
G	Y	U	N	I	V	E	S	R
E	N	R	S	G	U	V	I	Y
N	G	V	E	R	S	U	Y	I
U	R	E	G	Y	I	S	V	N
I	S	Y	V	U	N	G	R	E
S	E	I	Y	N	G	R	U	V
Y	V	N	U	S	R	I	E	G
R	U	G	I	V	E	Y	N	S

Word: **SURVEYING**

W	A	E	M	T	R	O	L	K
K	R	O	W	L	A	T	E	M
M	T	L	O	E	K	R	W	A
T	O	A	E	M	W	L	K	R
E	W	M	K	R	L	A	O	T
L	K	R	A	O	T	E	M	W
O	E	K	T	A	M	W	R	L
A	L	W	R	K	O	M	T	E
R	M	T	L	W	E	K	A	O

Word: **METALWORK**

32. Relax with a drink

C	I	T	N	A	E	R	U	O
E	O	N	R	U	T	I	A	C
R	A	U	O	C	I	T	E	N
N	T	E	U	O	C	A	R	I
O	U	R	A	I	N	C	T	E
A	C	I	T	E	R	O	N	U
U	R	C	E	T	O	N	I	A
I	N	A	C	R	U	E	O	T
T	E	O	I	N	A	U	C	R

Word: **COINTREAU**

F	A	E	P	L	O	N	I	T
L	O	I	N	A	T	F	E	P
T	N	P	F	E	I	O	A	L
E	P	O	A	T	N	L	F	I
I	L	F	O	P	E	T	N	A
N	T	A	I	F	L	E	P	O
O	F	L	E	I	A	P	T	N
A	E	T	L	N	P	I	O	F
P	I	N	T	O	F	A	L	E

Word: **PINT OF ALE**

Find out more

If you wish to improve your techniques for solving sudoku puzzles, I recommend that you read this book's companion volume, Robin Wilson's *How to Solve Sudoku: A Step-by-Step Guide*, published by Infinite Ideas. (ISBN 1-904902-62-6).

Many websites contain information about sudoku – http://en.wikipedia.org/wiki/Sudoku from *Wikipedia*, the free encyclopedia, is particularly informative and is updated regularly.

Finally, it only remains to wish you all the best with your sudoku explorations in the future.

Happy puzzling!